TEAMWORK
PLAYBOOK

FELLOWSHIP OF CHRISTIAN ATHLETES

TEAMWORK
PLAYBOOK

← ————————————

**TRUE CHAMPIONS TALK ABOUT
THE HEART AND SOUL IN SPORTS**

———————————— →

Revell
a division of Baker Publishing Group
Grand Rapids, Michigan

© 2016 by Fellowship of Christian Athletes

Published by Revell
a division of Baker Publishing Group
P.O. Box 6287, Grand Rapids, MI 49516–6287
www.revellbooks.com

Material adapted from *Teamwork*, published in 2009 by Regal Books

ISBN 978-0-8007-2692-8

Printed in the United States of America

16 17 18 19 20 21 22   7 6 5 4 3 2 1

Contents

The Four Core

DAN BRITTON

*Executive Vice President of
International Ministry, Fellowship
of Christian Athletes*

The NCAA Final Four tournament is an exciting sporting event. Even if you are not a person who likes basketball, it is awesome to watch March Madness as it narrows down sixty-four teams into four core teams. This makes me think about Fellowship of Christian Athlete's "Four Core"—not four core teams, but four core values.

Core values are simply the way you live and conduct yourself. They are your attitudes, beliefs, and convictions. Values should be what you are, not what you want to become. The goal is to embody your values every step of the way.

Are your values just words, or do you actually live them out? Can others identify the values in your life without your telling them? Your values need to be a driving force that shapes the way you do life! Talk is cheap, but values are valuable.

When everything is stripped away, what is left? For FCA, it is integrity, serving, teamwork, and excellence. These Four Core are so powerful to me that I have made them my own personal values. So, I have to ask you, what are your values? What guides you? Let me share with you FCA's Four Core, which are even better than the Final Four!

Integrity

To have integrity means that you are committed to Christlike wholeness, both privately and publicly. Basically, it means to live without gaps. Proverbs 11:3 says that integrity should guide you, but that a double life will destroy you. You need to be transparent, authentic, honest, and trustworthy. You should be the same in all situations and not become someone different when the competition of the game begins. Integrity means to act the same when no one is looking as you do when all eyes are on you. It is not about being perfect, but, as a coach or athlete, you need to be the real deal.

Serving

In John 13:12–15, Jesus gives us the perfect example of serving when He washes the disciples' feet. He then commands the disciples to go and do unto others what He has done to them. How many of your teammates' feet have you washed? Maybe not literally, but spiritually, do you have an attitude of serving just as if you were washing their feet in the locker room? You need to seek out the needs of others and be passionate about pursuing people who are needy. And, the last time I checked, everyone is needy.

Teamwork

Teamwork means to work together with others and express unity in Christ in all of your relationships. In Philippians 2:1–5, Paul encourages each of us to be one, united together in spirit and purpose. We all need to be on one team—not just the team we play on, but on God's Team! We need to equip, encourage, and empower one another. Do you celebrate and hurt together as teammates? You need to be arm-in-arm with others, locking up together to accomplish God's work. There should be no Lone Rangers.

Excellence

To pursue excellence means to honor and glorify God in everything you do. In Colossians 3:23–24, Paul writes, "whatever you do, work at it with all your heart, as working for the Lord, not for human masters" (NIV). The "whatever" part is hard, because it means that everything you do must be done for God, not others. You need to pursue excellence in practice, in games, in schoolwork and in lifting weights. God deserves your best, not your leftovers.

It is tip-off time for the game of life. How will you be known?

> Whatever happens, conduct yourselves in a manner worthy of the gospel of Christ.
>
> Philippians 1:27 NIV

Introduction

Me Monsters

Everyone should look out not only for his own interests, but also for the interests of others. Make your own attitude that of Christ Jesus.

Philippians 2:4–5

Lord Jesus, my prayer is to live and compete with integrity, serving, teamwork, and excellence. It is a high standard, but I know that with Your power and strength, it can happen. I want all my relationships to be known for things that are of You. Search my heart and reveal to me my values. I lay at the foot of the cross the values that do not honor You, and I ask for Your forgiveness. The values that bring You glory, I lay them at the foot of the cross for Your anointing.

One of my all-time favorite stand-up comedians has a routine about what he calls the "Me Monster"—the kind of person who is completely lost in his or her own world, consumed with his or her own desires, and who does all the talking for everyone else. Me Monsters are everywhere, especially in the athletic world. They lurk in every sport, on every team, in every organization. They are completely self-absorbed and focused on themselves instead of their team. In fact, they are enemies of true teamwork.

I'll never forget my first encounter with a teammate who was a Me Monster. He was a member of my college lacrosse team. I'd played with self-centered guys who didn't care about the team, but I'd never before met a full-blown Me Monster.

Now, when I talk about Me Monsters, I don't mean the kind of ball hogs we all know who never pass to their teammates. I'm not even talking about the ones who brag about their accomplishments and think that they are incredible athletes. I'm talking about the players who, after a brutal loss, are excited because they scored their goals. That's how my teammate felt. His excitement about how well he played and what he did on the field as an individual was evident, regardless of the team's performance. And if we won a big game and he didn't score or play well, he would be visibly upset in the locker room. He flat-out did not care about the team and was not the least bit concerned about teamwork. He was happy only when he played well as an individual.

This guy had incredible skills as a lacrosse player. Yet because of his selfish pursuits, he was not a great player. He wasn't even a good player. He was a dangerous player who broke down teamwork and the trust and loyalty within the team.

God taught me a lot through this teammate. Through his example, I realized how much of the same selfish nature was in me, and the Lord showed me that I needed less of me in me and more of Jesus in me. As humans, we speak more than nine million words a year. Half of them, statistics show, are possessive: "I," "me," "my," and "mine." I don't know about you, but I'm sick of talking and thinking about myself. And maybe, just maybe, others feel the same way, especially when it comes to teamwork.

In order to maintain healthy team dynamics, we all have to be aware of our own Me Monster tendency. In life, "we" is more powerful than "me," especially when it comes to teamwork. My college lacrosse teammate lived by the me-rather-than-we philosophy, which could just as well be the me-rather-than-He [Jesus] concept. And unfortunately, sports are usually all about the "me." As a coach, an athlete, or a leader, it is hard to die to self every day. But that is the only way God's best can be achieved. Think of how great it would be to have a team of "we"-focused athletes instead of those who are "me" focused.

Living out the concept of teamwork is to say, "We did it!" God can best use us when we sacrifice our own interests. He calls us to pick up our cross daily and follow Him. The popular acronym TEAM isn't found in Scripture, but you can't help but realize that it certainly applies: Together Everyone Achieves More.

How to Use This Book

Teamwork Playbook takes an in-depth look at this core value and comes at it from six different angles as lived out by six different people. Their insights shed new light on this value and give us a model to follow.

You can read *Teamwork Playbook* individually or as part of a group. As part of a personal devotion time, you can gain insight as you read through each story and ponder the "Training Time" questions at the end. Mentors can also use this book in a discipleship relationship, using the "Training Time" questions to step up conversations to the next level. And small groups (Huddles) can study the core value as a group to be prepared to sharpen each other with questions.

1

Losing Control

MIKE FISHER
NHL Defender

Trust in the LORD with all your heart, and do not rely on your own understanding; think about Him in all your ways, and He will guide you on the right paths.

Proverbs 3:5–6

Leadership is an act of submission to God. To be a leader means listening to all kinds of people and situations. Out of that listening, we are hoping to discern the mind of God as best we can. This is the price of leadership—it's an act of sacrifice. So leadership is part and parcel of the work of submission to God.

Richard Foster

Most great athletes instinctively want to take control. It's usually these athletes who rise to leadership roles within a team. But the best teams typically have leaders who understand that even they aren't really in control—and that's a good thing.

Since fully surrendering his heart to Christ at the age of twenty-two, NHL defender Mike Fisher has been intentionally and deliberately taking the steps toward a more trusting relationship with God. As a boy growing up in Peterborough, Ontario, he remembers coming downstairs before school every day and seeing his mom reading her Bible and spending time in prayer.

"Both my parents are prayer warriors," Fisher says. "They have a lot of faith in God, and that was a great example of what it looks like to trust God for direction. They knew they needed His guidance to lead our family."

Fisher's trust in God was first put to the test when he was nineteen years old. While playing juniors hockey, he suffered his first serious knee injury and had to sit out the remainder of the season.

"Remember, God doesn't make mistakes," his mother told him. "Trust in Him and it will be okay. He'll use it for good."

At the time, Fisher admits he wasn't terribly receptive to her advice. But in the long run, he knew she was right.

"I'll never forget some of those moments," he says.

Fisher's ability to trust God and let Him lead has made a difference in the way he has approached his hockey career. Fisher made his NHL debut with the Ottawa Senators in 2000 where he spent the better part of eleven seasons. It was an opportunity to be an example of his faith in a world where outspoken Christian athletes are a rarity. But Fisher sees that changing.

"Hockey has come a long way—even over the last ten years," he explains. "You're seeing more Christians emerging and there are some great chapel programs through Hockey Ministries International. But for me, it's just trying to be real. I've been in the league for a while and the first few years were probably the toughest. But after that, for the most part, the guys have come to respect that it's part of who I am. If you're truly living the way Jesus lived, then you're going to get those people that disagree. But you're also going to get those people who, if you're loving them the right way and you're being a good teammate, are going to respect you too."

But nowhere has Fisher found more divine camaraderie than within his own home. In 2010, Fisher married country music star Carrie Underwood, and the two continued a team-oriented approach that began with their dating relationship.

"Before we got married, trust was one of the three things our pastor touched on in our counseling," he says. "It's really second in importance only behind your relationship with Christ. We both live different lives and we're on the road a lot. We trust each other with all our hearts. It makes it so much easier to know I can trust her character and who she is as a person. That's the same way it is with the Lord. It's comforting. It's freeing. It brings a lot of peace knowing that you don't have to worry about anything and you can trust in Him. If you don't have that, good luck."

Just as a team captain has to take charge on the ice, Fisher feels a sobering sense of responsibility when it comes to serving as the leader of his marriage.

"I take it very seriously," he says. "We're both doing this thing together, but I understand that it's my job to make sure we're encouraging each other and praying together and growing spiritually. That's such an important thing. The closer we feel to God, the closer we feel to each other. When we're in the Word and growing and doing things we need to be doing, it makes the relationship so much better.

That's so important and it's a top priority in our marriage."

Fisher, who added fatherhood to his growing list of leadership titles in February of 2015, knows that the way he models character and trust in his marriage serves as an example for his teammates who look to him for leadership as one of the team's veterans. This has especially been true since he joined the Nashville Predators midway through the 2010–11 season.

"I've been able to be an example for the married guys and those guys that aren't even married yet," Fisher says. "Before I was married, I wanted to show them God's way to date properly and how to do the right things. I've gone through all that. I've been on the wrong side of it and done it the wrong way and fortunately with my wife, we did it the right way and God has really blessed that. That's allowed me to help some other guys along the way. It's all part of being a leader."

Fisher has also had ample opportunity to show his teammates what it looks like to trust God when things aren't going well. Through some shoulder and knee injuries, he has admittedly dealt with frustration and fear. It didn't take long for Fisher to realize that he had gotten off track and needed to completely surrender the situation to the Lord. In doing so, he began leaning heavily upon one of his favorite Scriptures: "Trust in the Lord with all your heart, and do not rely on your own understanding; think about Him in all your ways, and He will guide you on the right paths" (Prov. 3:5–6).

"A lot of times we hope that everything is going to be rosy, but God doesn't promise that," Fisher says. "He promises that He's got our back and He's prepared a place for us. We need to keep that perspective that it's not just about the here and now. That's exciting. We know we're going to go through ups and downs and we've all experienced that, but it's about surrendering some of that control, which we all find so hard to do, but it's really freeing when you can do that."

When doing his best to give up control and use biblical principles as a leader, Fisher believes that the only way to do that effectively is to follow Christ's perfect example.

"His ministry was showing love to others and trying to spread the gospel so people would trust in Him and have that faith," Fisher says. "What He did on the cross was the ultimate display of trust. He surrendered Himself to the cross because He knew that's what He needed to do. He sacrificed for us and He knew that God would raise Him up. Jesus gave up control on the cross and that's what the Lord wants us to do in a lot of areas in life. We know how hard that is, but imagine being in Jesus's position."

Fisher is no different than anyone else. His human nature craves control. But his advice for athletes and coaches and anyone who might struggle with this concept of leading under God's influence is to start with the little things and realize that it's a process that will take time.

"It's freeing when you start to give up some of that control," Fisher says. "But ultimately the most important decision you can make is giving your life over to Christ and trusting Him with it. That's an amazing thing. When you can do that, your fears begin to fade. What better person to have on your team than the God who made you?"

Training Time

1. Who are some people that you trust and why?

2. What are some areas of your life that you have struggled to turn over to God? What do you think has been the source of your lack of trust?

3. In what ways do you think trusting God can make someone a better

leader? How might that kind of leadership improve the team dynamic?

4. Read Proverbs 3:5–6. What parts
of that Scripture challenge you the
most?

5. What are some things you can start
to do today that will help you trust
God?

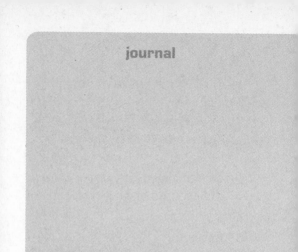

journal

journal

journal

2

Locking Arms

JUSTIN MASTERSON
MLB Pitcher

Iron sharpens iron, and one man sharpens another.

Proverbs 27:17

Fellowship means among other things that we are ready to receive of Christ from others. Other believers minister Christ to me, and I am ready to receive.

Watchman Nee

Justin Masterson is aware of the stigma that comes from growing up as a preacher's kid. But somewhere between the stereotypical Goody Two-shoes and unrepentant rebel lies the truth about what it's really like to be raised in a ministry home. While Masterson may not be able to pinpoint his exact location on that broad spectrum, he does know that having a pastor for a dad was nothing short of an incredible experience.

"I'm so thankful for that influence in my life," Masterson says. "I've been blessed to have a relationship with God since I was a little kid."

Masterson learned at a young age the importance of locking arms with those around him. It started in the home, but as an aspiring young athlete, he certainly became familiar with the oft-quoted Scripture found in Philippians 4:13: "I can do all things through Christ who strengthens me" (NKJV).

It was later in life when he had a revelation about this commonly misinterpreted passage.

"As the apostle Paul was writing that letter, he was physically in his weakest state," Masterson says. "He wasn't talking about how he could do anything he wanted to do like lift a boulder or something like that. He was saying that when you're mentally and emotionally at your weakest, Christ is going to be there for you. He will give you the strength. That's been a motto for me. I know I can still call on God to get through whatever hardship there might be."

Hardships are one thing Masterson can usually count on as a pitcher in the Major Leagues—there are plenty of down moments to accompany the occasional highlights. Locking arms with Jesus has helped him deal with disappointments and allowed him to appreciate his accomplishments even more. It also brings a sobering sense of perspective.

"I could have woken up today, maybe slept on my arm wrong, and never be able to pitch again," Masterson says. "If I'm not okay with that, then for me, I think that would be a problem. Not that I don't want to play anymore, but there are so many more important things to me than the game of baseball. There's my faith and my wife and my family. But for me it's just appreciating every day that you're given."

Masterson's wisdom on the subject of success and failure often opens the door to some interesting conversations with teammates about consistency.

"A player gets a hit and you always see him on first base hitting his chest and pointing to the sky," Masterson says. "But when he struck out last time, you didn't see him do that. It's true. It's not that you're excited that you struck out but you should thank the Lord that you had the chance to strike out. Some people may not totally understand that concept, but it's just as important to be thankful for the opportunity. I'm here. I'm breathing. I'm alive. That's especially important to remember in the hard times. If I give up the game-winning home run, I'm not the first to do that and I won't be the last. I just have to come back the next day and do what I know to do."

Masterson understands that there's a fine line between maintaining a win-at-all-costs attitude versus a lackadaisical attitude toward performance and results. It's been a journey of discovery for the Jamaican-born American. Masterson debuted with Boston during the 2008 season and went 6–5 with a respectable 3.16 earned run average. But midway through his second year, he was traded to Cleveland, where he hit a rough patch that resulted in a 7–20 record over the next season and a half.

His ability to stay even-keeled during those struggles paid off with especially solid seasons in 2011 and 2013. The latter resulted in Masterson's first All-Star Game appearance. Then in 2014, he was traded to St. Louis during the season and enjoyed success during the Cardinals' playoff run that went all the way to the National League Championship Series.

But no matter the outcome of any particular game or season, he wholeheartedly believes that it's important for him to model a balanced approach when it comes to winning and losing.

"If someone were to watch me throughout a season, they would know that every
single time I go out on the mound, they're
going to get the best that I have on that
day," Masterson says. "There's no way
they can think I don't care. In order to
continue to be at that level day after day,
you can't dwell on the bad things that
happen because that leads to an inability
to move on."

Ironically, Masterson has often been
misperceived as someone who lacks that
competitive fire due to his laid-back per-
sonality. For his teammates, that changes
quickly when they see him pitch. No longer does he appear to simply be someone who is happy to be alive; instead he
displays a ferocious side on the mound
and a desire to do everything to the best
of his ability.

That drive isn't limited to his baseball
career. Masterson believes he must also
put equal, if not greater, effort into his
Christian walk. Bible study and prayer are

key, but so is fellowship with believers. This is something to which Masterson can especially relate as someone who participates in a team sport at the professional level.

"When I'm pitching, I can't always identify what I'm doing wrong," Masterson says. "But it's usually the coaches and the other players who are watching me who might be able to see those things that I can't see or feel."

The key, however, is being receptive to constructive criticism and applying that helpful advice to the situation. Masterson understands that a close relationship with his coaches and teammates can only make him better. The same rings true as a spiritual principle.

"What goes in your ears and into your mind is what's going to come out," he says. "That's why you need to have the quality inputs going into your head. You need to have the Word of God going into your heart. It's good to read on your own and have a personal study time, but there's a sense of community when you have some time with other believers. It's really easy to feel like you're alone—like you're the only Christian, the only person believing. Then you can start falling into the paths that aren't good because you don't notice it."

Masterson likens it to the Casting Crowns' song "Slow Fade," which features lyrics that describe how easy it can be to fall away from a vibrant relationship with God when that fellowship is not maintained.

"I need another set of eyes, someone I can talk to and bounce things off and really dig deeper with because more than likely they'll come from a different perspective," he says. "That's something you've got to have because that's what helps you to grow stronger and become closer to God."

In the Old Testament, King Solomon made a sage observation that is just as true today as it was thousands of years ago: "Iron sharpens iron, and one man sharpens another" (Prov. 27:17).

The apostles likewise understood this divinely inspired principle. Paul reminded the early Christians in Thessalonica to "encourage one another and build each other up" (1 Thess. 5:11) while the apostle James exhorted believers to take it a step further and "confess your sins to one another and pray for one another" (James 5:16).

Those are the actions of a body that is locking arms while standing shoulder to shoulder and walking a shared path toward a more Christ-centered life. Not only does Masterson feel passionately about the need to share the lessons he has learned with fellow Christians but he also seeks to put those things into action as an expression of what Jesus taught in Matthew 22:37–39.

"I love that passage because Jesus tells us plain and simple that he wants us to love God with all we are and to love people," he says. "If you do those things, your mind and will and actions will be moving in the right direction toward God."

And for Masterson, that's ultimately what playing professional baseball is all about—being a light for Christ.

"I'm trying to live out what Jesus has called me to do," he says. "I want to take the opportunities I'm given to share with people why I'm so happy and why my life is so great. It's because I have Jesus in my life. I want to build up Christ and show who He really is. And then the Holy Spirit will do the work in their heart. You build Christ up and then it's just taking the opportunity if it's there. That's why I'm happy to be here, so I can proclaim His name."

Training Time

1. What comes to mind when you hear the phrase "locking arms"?

2. Who are some people with whom you have locked arms? How did that support impact you?

3. Can you think of a time when you didn't have that kind of support in your life?

4. Describe the differences between the two scenarios.

5. How do you think that locking arms with like-minded believers might help you more effectively live out the commands that Jesus gave in Matthew 22:37–39?

journal

3

Know (and Accept) Your Role

CAT WHITEHILL

*Former US Women's Soccer Team
Defender and Olympic Gold Medalist*

Now you are the body of Christ,
and individual members of it.

1 Corinthians 12:27

I am a member of a team, and I
rely on the team, I defer to it and
sacrifice for it, because the team,
not the individual, is the ultimate
champion.

Mia Hamm

Cat Whitehill knows a little something
about dynasties. She played for the University
of North Carolina soccer program,
which through 2014 has accumulated 21
of 33 NCAA titles—including championships
in 2000 and 2003 (Whitehill's freshman
and senior seasons at Chapel Hill).
Throughout the 2000s, Whitehill was also
a mainstay on the historically dominant
US National Team.

Even back in her home state of Alabama, she was part of a club team that claimed five state titles, four of them with Whitehill on board. So it's not surprising that Whitehill, a self-proclaimed sports junkie, grew up being inspired by dynasties—even if they weren't always in the same sport.

"You look at Michael Jordan and how incredible he was at the game of basketball," Whitehill says. "And then you look at Scottie Pippen and see that he was an incredible player too, but so many people forget about him and Dennis Rodman and Horace Grant and Steve Kerr and B. J. Armstrong. They all made the Bulls become one of the greatest dynasties of my era. None of those players cared that Michael Jordan was as great as he was because Michael Jordan cared about how his team won. That's what makes someone become the greatest."

Born in Virginia but raised in Birmingham, Alabama, Whitehill came by her love of sports honestly. Her father, Phil Reddick, played football at Virginia Tech and would toss around the pigskin with his daughters, Cat and Virginia. But that's not the only way Reddick was influential in Whitehill's life. His roles as associate pastor at Briarwood Presbyterian Church and, more importantly, as spiritual leader of the home played a significant part in Whitehill's devotion to God.

"Because I come from a Christian family, it was ingrained in my head from day one," Whitehill says. "When I was five years old, I accepted Christ into my life. I remember I was sleeping on my trundle bed one night, and my parents and I prayed together. When you're five years old, you just do what your parents do, and I had different situations where I could've chosen another path, but God just made sense. I've grown in Him, and I came from a Christian school where I received an incredible knowledge of the Bible and the history of Christ."

From the outside looking in, Whitehill admits many are likely to hold preconceived notions about her upbringing. She enjoys busting the myths that for years have accompanied those who grew up in households that were overtly churchgoing and ministry-oriented.

"When you hear that I'm a preacher's kid, you might think I'm the rebellious kind," Whitehill says. "But my family allowed me to choose, and they never forced their views on me. Both my sister and I are so grateful for that, because never once did either of us stray from our faith. It just clicked with both of us. Obviously, there have been ups and downs in my career and ups and downs in my personal life, but having God in my life is what's kept my head above water."

Whitehill has also benefited greatly from her family's close-knit nature. One of the many lessons she learned from her father was that "you can always help your teammate be better." In fact, Whitehill has grown to love the feeling that comes from helping someone improve in his or her abilities—especially when no one else ever knows.

"Teamwork is putting your personal preferences aside and looking at the person on your right and the person on your left first," Whitehill says. "It's putting aside everything in your personal life and your athletic career and doing whatever it takes to make someone else better. In turn, if you're going to make them better, they have to decide that they want to make you better."

Whitehill admittedly gets frustrated—as an athlete and as a sports fan—when she sees high-profile athletes blatantly put their selfish desires in front of their team's goals. "People describe certain athletes as great team players, but sometimes when the spotlight is shining on you, it's easy to forget about teamwork," Whitehill says. "But it's important to remember that you can't do it alone. When you put others first, it just makes the game a lot more fun, and it makes playing the game a whole lot easier."

While Whitehill was learning the finer art of traditional teamwork at UNC, she met, fell in love with, and on December 31, 2005, married her husband, Robert. Their venture as a couple has opened her eyes to a whole new element of the team concept.

"I'm not just one person anymore," Whitehill says. "There's a lot more compromise that comes with marriage. I can't just make a decision and have that be the end. I have to go to Robert, and we have to talk it out. It's a great learning experience for me, because I'm a pretty stubborn person. When we come together and make a decision, that's really cool. It's the same thing when you come together as a team, and you make a decision or you win a game. I think you get so much more out of it than if you were to do it by yourself."

The same can be said for Whitehill's involvement on the US National Team. She has learned a great deal about compromise and unity from her vast international experience. Whitehill played for the Under-16 National Team in 1998 as well as the Under-18 squad from 1998 to 2000. She played a key role at the 1999 Pan American Games, leading the United States to a gold medal with a spectacular long-distance goal in the championship match against Mexico.

With the Under-21 National Team, Whitehill was a starter and an invaluable contributor as the US squad collected four consecutive Nordic Cup titles from 2000 to 2003 (five consecutive titles, dating back to 1999).

On July 7, 2000, Whitehill made her first appearance on the women's National Team against Italy and has been a contributor as both a starter and key bench reserve ever since. At the 2004 Summer Olympic Games in Athens, she started three of the five games as the US women claimed the gold medal. She also made headlines by filling in for the injured Brandi Chastain during the 2003 World Cup, where the team finished in third place.

"The standard is very high," Whitehill says. "It's high in the way that you play the game. It's high in your mental capacity. The standard is high everywhere. If you were a star in high school and you come to a team like North Carolina or if you were a star in college and you come to one of these national teams, you're going to be humbled. You're not going to be the star anymore."

And even as team oriented as the majority of the national team's athletes have been, there's always the potential for self-serving motives to be lurking around the corner. Perhaps, Whitehill suggests, that's why winning under those circumstances (with the country's elite players all gathered together) is that much more special.

"We're all a bunch of type-A females, but when we compromise and we come together as a team, then we can use our abilities to make the team so great," she says. "It's having the ability but also figuring out that we're a team, and we're not just a bunch of individuals."

Maybe it's because of the way her father ingrained certain principles into her head as she was growing up. Maybe it's because of her passion for college and professional team sports. Or maybe it's because of the personal experiences she has accrued over a lifetime of playing soccer at the highest level. Most likely, however, Whitehill's desire to put the team first in all situations is the result of a combination of all of the above.

"Teamwork has been easy for me," she says. "I just love watching sports, and I love watching the details of sports. I just want to win. I have this strong desire to win. If I need to push my teammates into the goal with the ball, I will do it. I will do whatever it takes. I know I can't do it alone. I want to win so badly that I will do whatever it takes for my teammates to get better."

Arguably, the teamwork concept has not always been emphasized within the walls of most churches. But Whitehill believes this foundational principle is clearly taught throughout both the Old and New Testaments. "You can see teamwork throughout the whole Bible," she says. "There wasn't just one disciple—there were twelve. Each one had an incredible quality about them. You see the idea of people working together for a common goal all over the Bible, but sometimes you don't think of it as teamwork."

One of the more obvious representations of teamwork can be found in 1 Corinthians 12, where the apostle Paul compares the body of Christ to the human body. In verses 27–31, he addresses the issue of different roles that Christians play in order for the church to be successful

in its mission of bringing the unsaved to
salvation:

> Now you are the body of Christ, and
> individual members of it. And God has
> placed these in the church: first apostles,
> second prophets, third teachers, next
> miracles, then gifts of healing, helping,
> managing, various kinds of languages.
> Are all apostles? Are all prophets? Are
> all teachers? Do all do miracles? Do all
> have gifts of healing? Do all speak in
> other languages? Do all interpret? But
> desire the greater gifts. And I will show
> you an even better way.

Paul is letting all believers know that
there is a place for everyone on God's
team; and each position, or role, is just
as vital as the next. "The bench is just
as important as the people on the field,"
Whitehill says. "I've had a lesson in both.
I've been on the bench and I've been on
the field. God always has a plan, and
whether I'm on the bench or on the field,

He wants me to be in that role. For me, the role is important, because I can show Christ through that role. If I'm a bench player, I can be okay with that. It's not where I want to be, but I can push the other defenders and make them better. If their line is off, I can tell them, because I have a much better perspective. If I'm on the field, I want someone on the bench to do the same thing for me."

But true to form, the all-too-common human element of pride eventually works its way into the mix. Selfish motives—whether driven by insecurity or arrogance—cause people (and especially athletes) to question their station in life or on a team. King Solomon wisely pegged this wrong way of thinking in Proverbs 21:2: "All a man's ways seem right to him, but the LORD evaluates the motives."

"Everyone thinks they should be on the field," Whitehill says. "They don't see through the eyes of the coach or the eyes of their teammates. They see through their own eyes. You're thinking, *I'm better than that player. Why am I not out there?* You're at a competitive level, so you are a great player. But for some reason, there's something that separates someone else from you on that day or maybe the coach just likes them better. There's a lot that comes into play, but the pride issue is huge. For someone who has a lot of pride, if they don't know their role, a lot of times they won't stay on the team."

Overcoming pride takes a solid understanding of who we are in Christ. Philippians 1:6 tells us that "He who started a good work in you will carry it on to completion until the day of Christ Jesus." In other words, anyone who is insecure about his or her ability and feels the need to achieve individual greatness in order to find security and self-worth can trust that our Creator has a plan that no amount of success in athletics or elsewhere can match.

Another great reminder can be found in Colossians 2:9–10: "For the entire fullness of God's nature dwells bodily in Christ, and you have been filled by Him, who is the head over every ruler and authority."

Both of those reassuring Scriptures help Whitehill stand confident in her faith, no matter what trials she may face on or off the field.

"Knowing who God is and knowing what God did for us is really important," Whitehill says. "It's important to love people in spite of what they may say to you, what they may do to you, or who they are and what they believe. That's who Christ was and that's who God wants us to be. My teammates know what I believe, and I know what they believe, and we can still be great teammates. I can still be a witness to them, because I'm not going to back down. I'm stubborn. They're not going to back down either, because they're stubborn; but in the end, it's really Christ who wins."

As important as it is for Cat White-hill to demonstrate godly teamwork to her teammates and to the greater soccer community and sports world, her desire to exercise this irreplaceable core value is also steeped in a solid understanding of just how powerful a difference a unified, fully functioning group of believers committed to excellence can truly make.

"We're a congregation," Whitehill says. "We are Christ's body. If we can remember that, teamwork just makes so much more sense. If we realize that we're representing Christ and the pastor is the one in the spotlight, we can just follow them and make the pastor greater, because of how we act and because of who we are as a congregation."

Whitehill, who most recently has starred in the National Women's Soccer League (NWSL) with the Boston Breakers, says some of her friends often ask why she still plays soccer after all of these years. In response, she usually refers to her love of the team and the love of learning new things on a daily basis. Whitehill also enjoys the opportunity to be a role model for young soccer players and sports fans of all ages throughout the entire country.

"I want them to know that we're not all going to be the Michael Jordans of this world," Whitehill says. "And if you are, the greatest thing you can do for someone is to build them up to be the best that they can be.

"So many people have this perception that you have to be Michael Jordan or Tiger Woods," she concludes. "Yes, they are excelling at their sports, but as humans we can excel to the best of our ability. That's what Christ wants, and that's what's important. That's what a great team wants—to get the best out of each other."

Training Time

1. Cat Whitehill references Michael Jordan and the Chicago Bulls as one of the greatest examples of

teamwork. What are some other dynasties that come to mind? What do you think are some of the key components of a sports dynasty at any level?

2. What are some of the roles you have played on a team? Have you ever felt as if your role wasn't as important as another player's role? Why do some positions in a group dynamic get more attention than others?

3. Read 1 Corinthians 12:12–31, in which Paul compares the church to a body. In your sport or team dynamic, how would you compare the various positions and roles to the parts of the human body? Have you had to compete or fulfill a task with someone missing? How did that impact the group's ability to succeed?

4. In what ways have you felt called to use your talents and gifts within the body of Christ? Have you ever felt as if your role was not important

or not significant? If so, explain. Read Philippians 1:6. How does this promise from God change any uncertainties you feel about God's call on your life?

5. What does true greatness in the spiritual sense mean to you? What are some ways that you can strive to be a great "teammate" within the body of Christ?

journal

4

Trust or Consequences

ANDY PETTITTE
Former MLB Pitcher

Never let loyalty and faithfulness leave you. Tie them around your neck; write them on the tablet of your heart. Then you will find favor and high regard in the sight of God and man.

Proverbs 3:3–4

Men of genius are admired. Men of wealth are envied. Men of power are feared. But only men of character are trusted.

Arthur Freidman

Trust is a funny thing. It takes years to build but can be destroyed in an instant. Trust requires honesty, communication, loyalty, and proven moral integrity. It is one of the foundational elements behind every great team.

Andy Pettitte knows all about the fragile nature of trust. He has spent his entire life building up trustworthy relationships with his family, his friends, his teammates, the baseball community, and the public at large. Yet a single seemingly insignificant misstep can open the door for doubt, which often then results in a certain measure of distrust. In today's society, it doesn't take much for a cynical public (and an even more cynical media) to question one's integrity and chip away at that bedrock of trust.

Pettitte found that fact to be all too true in December 2007 when his name was mentioned in the highly publicized *Mitchell Report*, the written results of an investigation led by former Senator George Mitchell into the prevalence of performance-enhancing drugs within Major League Baseball (MLB). The report and subsequent public statements made by Pettitte revealed that in 2002 and in 2004, Pettitte, in an attempt to recover from elbow injuries, had received injections of human growth hormone.

Even though the use of the human growth hormone was not illegal or banned by the MLB at the time, the onslaught of attention that followed (and the brutally negative reaction by some members of the press) caused the former New York Yankees' pitcher to think twice about continuing his career. Was subjecting his family to an invasion of privacy worth it? Was it fair to put his teammates through the media circus during spring training?

Having already signed a contract to play in 2008, Pettitte ultimately had one choice and one choice only. "I felt that [quitting] wouldn't be a very honorable thing to do; that wouldn't be a thing to do as a man," Pettitte told reporters on February 18, 2008. "I felt like I needed to come out and be forward with this. Whatever circumstances or repercussions come with it, I'll take it like a man, and I'll try to do my job."

That's because at his core, Pettitte is the best kind of teammate. He's the best kind of husband and father as well. He is a trustworthy man whose lifelong commitment to integrity cannot be shaken by the overreaction of the vocal minority who are always seeking to make mountains out of proverbial molehills. Pettitte understands that there is no such thing as perfection and that whether people trust you or not isn't always up to you anyway.

Those are just a few lessons about teamwork that he has learned over the years. Originally from Baton Rouge, Louisiana, Pettitte's family moved to Deer Park, Texas, when he was in the third grade. There, his baseball career flourished, and while he was pitching for Deer Park High School, he drew the attention of pro scouts. Although he was selected by the Yankees in the twenty-second round of the 1990 draft, the towering lefty decided to first attend San Jacinto College in Texas before signing with New York.

Pettitte played in Yankee pinstripes from 1995 to 2003 and was a part of four World Series championship teams. He then spent three years (2004–06) playing for the Houston Astros and led that club to its first World Series appearance in 2005, before returning to the Yankees in 2007.

Considered one of the most dominant postseason starting pitchers in the modern era, Pettitte ranks second among Louisiana-born pitchers in career wins (behind Ted Lyons's 260) and has never had a losing record.

But long before Pettitte was making a name for himself in the Fall Classic, the star athlete's education about teamwork began in a much different setting. Although he was raised in what he describes as a "very strong Catholic family," it was a fateful first visit to the church of his sister's friend that set the tone for his spiritual growth.

"I was eleven years old when I went with her one night," Pettitte says. "It was really the first time in my life that I heard about having a relationship with the Lord and heard that I needed Him as my personal Savior. That was the night that I accepted Jesus into my heart and was saved. I've felt like an absolutely different person since then."

About four years later, Pettitte began attending Central Baptist Church—the church that he still calls home today. It was there he met his wife, Laura. She was the daughter of the pastor (since retired), and her brothers were active in ministry there as well. Pettitte would eventually serve in various capacities at the church: teaching in Sunday school, singing in the choir, and mentoring teens, young adults, and young married couples.

As a young Christian athlete, Pettitte learned one of the most important lessons about teamwork, not on the baseball field but in his home and in his church, where strong men of faith taught him that trustworthy relationships are built on integrity.

"My dad was a man who always showed me love," Pettitte says. "It was tough love sometimes, but he always made time for me. If he told me he was going to do something, he would always do it for me. My father-in-law was a wonderful Christian man. He was just constantly in the Word. When I looked at him, I saw a man who just loved the Bible and was always studying the Word. My brother-in-law worked in the youth department at the church, and I was under him. I was around the Word and I was around Christian people, and these things were just constantly being instilled in me."

Pettitte also says his openness to the Holy Spirit was a key factor in those earliest inclinations toward a lifestyle of godly righteousness. "I was convicted to not drink," he says. "I was convicted to not use the Lord's name in vain. He took all the bad language away from me. I was just extremely convicted of these things at a very young age. I thank the Lord that He's kept His hands around me and protected me. I've had so many people praying for me. I think that's a huge reason why I've been able to live the life that I've lived. God's protection has just been on me."

Pettitte is especially thankful for his wife, Laura, whom he credits for the desire to pursue integrity and strive to be a faithful, trustworthy man. The couple has been acting as a team since they first met as teenagers and made a commitment to abstain from sex until they were married.

Pettitte truly believes that his wife is a mirror image of the woman written about by Solomon in Proverbs 31 and agrees wholeheartedly with verses 10–12: "Who can find a capable wife? She is far more precious than jewels. The heart of her husband trusts in her, and he will not lack anything good. She rewards him with good, not evil, all the days of her life."

Because Pettitte views his wife as a treasure and a gift from God, he has always been conscientious of any actions that could damage the bond of trust they have forged over the years. While many athletes often struggle with the temptations that lurk around every corner, Pettitte says that for him the exact opposite has been true.

"It hasn't been that difficult for me, because I have kept myself away from certain situations," he says. "A lot of people put themselves in bad situations; but we're human, and we're going to fall, and we're going to fail. Have there been opportunities for me to screw up? Of course there have. But you don't jeopardize your marriage and that trust. That's the biggest thing for me that I've always tried to do. Again, it's because I've been involved in the church, and I've seen what can happen, and I've seen people's lives ruined if you lose the trust of your spouse. It's going to be hard to get back, and it's hard to overcome. I just thank God that I haven't put myself in those situations where my wife would not trust me or would have doubts about me and my love for her."

While Pettitte doesn't hold an official position at his home church, the unofficial ministry he has done gives him a bird's-eye view of just how devastating those trust-busting mistakes can be on a marriage or in a family or even between friends. He's found this to be especially true when the loss of trust is caused by sexual activity that is contradictory to biblically sound doctrine.

"I think there are a lot of things that are carried into marriages when those individuals have been involved with other people," Pettitte explains. "A lot of people come to me, even though I'm not a minister. I think people know that I'll listen, and they can talk to me. I know a lot of people who have bad stuff going on in their marriages, and it's from things that happened before they were married. You're going to reap consequences from some bad decisions that you make in your life. All of us have made bad decisions in our lives, and usually you're going to reap some of that stuff. That's why it's so wonderful being a Christian, because you can ask God for forgiveness, and He forgives you of it."

As an athlete who was equally committed to teamwork and sharing his beliefs, Pettitte found that the trust between him and his teammates often opened the door for him to counsel them on relationship issues. It's a direct reflection of the promise found in Proverbs 3:3–4: "Never let loyalty and faithfulness leave you. Tie them around your neck; write them on the tablet of your heart. Then you will find favor and high regard in the sight of God and man."

"I have always had a unique opportunity to reach out to my teammates," Pettitte says. "I don't try to judge anybody. I just try to love them and encourage them. I always tell them that when you marry someone, I believe that it's for life. You should stick with your wife and figure out a way to get through it. I believe that's how God wants it, and I believe Satan wants every marriage destroyed and to break every family up. So it's given me a lot of opportunities. As you can imagine, in baseball, a lot of guys are screwing up and doing a lot of wrong things. I try to be as genuine as I can, and I thank the Lord that guys will share stuff with me and open up with me when things happen. I think they just know that I'm going to love them, and I'm going to pray for them."

But none of these opportunities to share God's love with others would be possible if it weren't for Pettitte's desire to emulate Jesus. He understands and embraces the fact that to be a good teammate requires the same level of trust and respect as it does for him to be a good family man and a good friend. His belief is backed up by what Jesus taught in Matthew 5:37: "Let your word 'yes' be 'yes,' and your 'no' be 'no.' Anything more than this is from the evil one."

Says Pettitte, "Whenever you say you're going to do something, you do it. There are a lot of people in the world today whose word doesn't mean a whole lot. If that's where you're at, then I don't think you're showing a whole lot of integrity. Nobody's perfect, and we're all going to screw up, and we're all going to mess up. But that's how we should try to live our lives. If I tell my children I'm going to do something, I need to be the kind of father who's going to back it up and try to do that for them."

This principle carries over to Pettitte's professional life as well, and in particular is something he strives to maintain when dealing with his team's upper management. At the conclusion of the 2007 season, the Yankees put a one-year offer on the table for him to return in 2008. Pettitte, who has struggled with elbow issues for the past several years, asked for a player's option so that he wouldn't be forced to make a rushed decision but instead make a prayerful, wise choice.

"If I had signed a two-year contract with those guys, I would have felt obligated to come back and play for them," he explains. "Even if my arm hurt, I would just try to pitch through the pain. Well, they gave me an option, which means that if I felt like I was healthy, I could just activate the option. They trusted my word that if my arm was hurt, they believed that I wouldn't activate the option just to make the money that they were going to offer me. The Yankees showed a lot of faith in me with that situation, and I would hope they did that because they think I'm an honest man and that I would have the integrity to do the right thing. As a man, it made me feel good that they would say, 'Hey, Andy, we'll entrust this to you. We'll let you make this decision because we know you're not going to try to pull something over on us.'"

So when the *Mitchell Report* was re-
leased a week after he signed the contract,
it was no surprise that the entire Yankees organization rallied to support him.
When he met with the media at spring
training, he was flanked by manager
Joe Girardi and general manager Brian
Cashman. Sitting just a few feet away
were close friends and teammates Jorge
Posada, Derek Jeter, and Mariano Rivera.

Everyone in that clubhouse and in the
front office knew that Pettitte's rare lapse
in judgment was not a reflection of his
character. They knew how important
it was for him to have his teammates'
trust. The same was also true for his wife,
Laura, who stood by his side throughout
the entire process as he worked to restore
any trust that might have been lost.

And for that to happen, Pettitte will do
the same thing he did to build that trust
in the first place. He will be a faithful,
loyal, moral man and will continue to
reflect those values in every area of his

life—the ball field, the church, and, most importantly, his home. That's how Pettitte plans to maintain his standing as someone whom his teammates can count on long after his retirement.

"I'm big on relationships," Pettitte says. "I care about the guys on the team that I play with. I want to try to be a positive influence on my team—not just on the baseball field but in their lives. When I'm done playing and I walk away from this game, I hope that I've impacted somebody's life in a positive way."

Training Time

1. Have you ever made a mistake that caused someone to lose trust in you? What steps did you take to restore that trust between yourself and others?

2. What role does teamwork play when it comes to trustworthy relationships with a spouse, a family

member, a teammate, or a fellow Christian? Is it possible to be a successful team without trust?

3. Andy Pettitte says that he has "a unique opportunity to reach out to my teammates." What does their openness to his counsel say about the level of trust they have in his moral integrity? Who are some people that you go to for wise counsel? What about their character makes them excellent candidates for such a role in your life?

4. Pettitte tells a story about a time his team's management trusted him to make an honest and timely decision. Have you ever been in a similar situation? How was your word tested? How did the outcome affect your working relationship with those involved?

5. Read Proverbs 3:3–4. How important are loyalty and faithfulness within any given team dynamic?

What are some consequences when those values are absent? What are some ways that you can be more loyal, faithful, and trustworthy?

journal

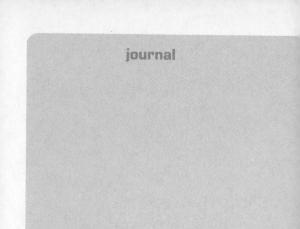

journal

5

Eyes on the Prize

LUKE RIDNOUR
NBA Guard

One thing I do: Forgetting what is behind and reaching forward to what is ahead, I pursue as my goal the prize promised by God's heavenly call in Christ Jesus.

Philippians 3:13–14

Destiny is not a matter of chance; it is a matter of choice. It is not a thing to be waited for; it is a thing to be achieved.

William Jennings Bryan

If you've never heard of Coeur d'Alene, Idaho, don't feel too bad. Even NBA point guard Luke Ridnour, the town's most famous product, wouldn't expect many people to know much (if anything) about his birthplace.

Although its population is anything but tiny, only those living in the northwestern

United States tend to know much about the city that sits along the edge of the scenic Coeur d'Alene National Forest. And it was in Coeur d'Alene that Ridnour first fell in love with the game of basketball. He lived there until he was seven years old and recalls attending a Christian school where his mother was a teacher.

"When I was in kindergarten, my dad used to play basketball with me at lunchtime against the third and fourth graders," Ridnour says. "That was my first memory of playing basketball. He was a coach, so he would come in and mess around with me and play two-on-two against the other kids."

Oddly enough, Ridnour and his family went even deeper into obscurity when they moved to Blaine, Washington, a town that sits in the state's extreme northwest corner and rests against the US-Canadian border. While there, he attended Blaine High School with about four hundred students and graduated with ninety seniors. The tight-knit community was extremely supportive of its athletic programs, which Ridnour led to a pair of state hoops titles. More important for him, however, was the development of his ideas about teamwork.

"Since I can remember, it was that same crew of guys playing together," he explains. "It was never about putting one guy in front of another guy. It was always about our team. We represented that community, and we weren't just playing for ourselves. That's the coolest thing I can remember—the loyalty we had toward each other. We didn't care who the star was. We just wanted to be there for each other and win."

Ridnour credits his father for providing the earliest lessons about teamwork. Rob Ridnour coached high-school basketball (including his son's team) before taking over as the head coach of the International Basketball League's Bellingham Slam. It was the elder Ridnour who instilled in his son some of those fundamental concepts about teamwork, such as sharing the ball and looking out for one another.

"The biggest thing my dad taught me about teamwork was that everyone should stick together through thick and thin," Ridnour says. "These are the guys you're going to be with, and no matter how bad it might look at times, that's your crew that you've got to pull together with. The guys who are on the court are the ones who have to get the job done. You can't look to other people. You've all got to do it together."

While pursuing his NBA dream, Ridnour says that maintaining a relationship with Christ was rarely a priority. He grew up in church, but his focus on athletics deterred him from taking a serious look at the faith his parents embraced. Still, he knew something was missing in his life. "As much success as I'd had, I wasn't very happy," Ridnour says. "I still didn't have very much peace about who I was. But once I hit college, God really spoke to my heart. He started drawing me closer and closer to Him. I started to find peace, and I got excited about the fact that I wasn't just a basketball player, but I was friends with Jesus. That's what really changed my life."

At the University of Oregon, Ridnour found strength and accountability in a group of freshmen teammates who were all experiencing similar spiritual growth patterns. They met together for Bible studies with team chaplain Keith Jenkins—a pastor from Eugene, Oregon—and faithfully attended a local church.

Ridnour says that fellowship opened his eyes "to the power of God and how real He is." Likewise, a growing comprehension of the Bible enhanced his understanding of and appreciation for the concept of teamwork.

"It's very much biblical with principles such as putting others before you,"

Ridnour says. "I think that's what teamwork is. A good teammate puts others before him. No one person thinks they're bigger than they really are. The Bible just reinforced the belief that I can't put myself above anybody else."

Ridnour is especially inspired by the words of the apostle Paul found in Romans 12:3: "For by the grace given to me, I tell everyone among you not to think of himself more highly than he should think. Instead, think sensibly, as God has distributed a measure of faith to each one." "I think that's huge for teamwork," Ridnour says. "A lot of times, you can be worried about yourself and your success. But when you put your team's success ahead of your success, good things happen."

Ridnour earned Pac-10 Player of the Year honors as a junior in 2002–03 and then made an early departure for the NBA, where he was the fourteenth overall selection of the Seattle SuperSonics.

After five seasons with the Sonics (a franchise that has since moved to Oklahoma City), he was traded to Milwaukee in a three-team, six-player deal and has also spent time with Minnesota, Charlotte, and Orlando. His experiences at the highest level of competition continue to bring revelation about the biblical principles of teamwork—despite the fact that so much of playing in the NBA is about the individual athletes and their desire to earn high-dollar contracts.

"But no matter what level you're at, the most important thing is still the team," Ridnour says. "My first responsibility is to make sure all of my decisions are going to help the team win the game. The second thing is making everybody else better. It's doing the little things like getting the ball into the right hands at the right time or even scoring at times when you have to."

As a point guard, another line item on Ridnour's checklist is taking care of the ball. And while he agrees that he needs to do everything he can to limit turnovers, he also says that he must avoid the trap of thinking too much about it. "You can't be afraid to make mistakes," Ridnour says. "If you look at some of the great point guards, they were never afraid to take a risk on a pass. For me, being a point guard also means showing your creative side and having the freedom to go out and do what God's called me to do and have fun doing it. I don't really worry about turnovers. I know it's an important part of the game, but as you play more, you get more confident and don't turn the ball over as much."

For Ridnour to be truly successful at his craft, he must have impeccable vision, or what others often refer to as court awareness. He needs to hone that innate ability to see the big picture and all of its finest details. "For me, good vision is about instinct," he says. "It's about knowing your teammates: what they can do and what they can't do. It's also about knowing the game. When I'm leading a fast break, I have a good idea of where everybody is at, and they might not even be there yet. Then you just let your instincts take over. When I try to force it, that's when turnovers happen. But when you let your instincts go and play freely, you might not see it, but it happens."

Ridnour equates his vision as a point guard to his vision as a follower of Christ. He fully understands the vital nature of having a clear picture of God's will for his life and the ultimate prize that comes with a personal relationship with Jesus. But as a young athlete, Ridnour admits that until he reached college, he didn't always have the vision necessary to see what was around him. He didn't realize what kind of impact he could have on others as a man of faith.

"When God started to open up my eyes and let me see things through His eyes, I could see that there were so many people around me who I could touch," Ridnour says. "It's a daily thing. You can influence and touch so many people just by being around them and saying the right things and being there for them. We get so caught up in day-to-day stuff, but as far as eternity is concerned, we need to keep our eyes on the big picture. So when adversity comes, it's really not that big of a deal when we look at what we have coming."

For Ridnour, this promise for the future is found in Philippians 3:20–21: "Our citizenship is in heaven, from which we also eagerly wait for a Savior, the Lord Jesus Christ. He will transform the body of our humble condition into the likeness of His glorious body, by the power that enables Him to subject everything to Himself."

Having that knowledge of eternal glory along with the understanding that we can have a vibrant relationship with Jesus in this lifetime has helped Ridnour grasp the more personal aspects of teamwork—even as it relates to interactions with his peers off the court. "One of the biggest things a point guard needs to do is have relationships with his teammates," he says. "Whether they're your kind of people or not, it's important not to just get along but to have a sincere relationship with all of the players and coaches. That makes a difference on and off the court. On the court, it's our job to make everybody better and to do that they need to listen to you and respect you."

It took Ridnour a little bit longer to learn how that truth applied to his fellowship with believers. He admits that he once had tunnel vision and would think of himself long before he would think about others. Then he came across the admonition found in Galatians 6:2, where Paul tells us to "carry one another's burdens; in this way you will fulfill the law of Christ."

"One of the things I used to find myself doing in prayer was only praying about my needs," Ridnour remembers. "'Lord, I need this. Lord, I need that.' But God calls us to pray for all the saints. We're supposed to pray for our spouses, our families, and our friends. We're supposed to pray for the salvation of people around us. And once you find yourself praying for other people, you start to see your own prayers answered."

From there, Ridnour began to get a clearer picture of what teamwork should look like within the body of Christ. He made rich discoveries within the pages of God's Word, including a promise given by Jesus in Matthew 18:19–20: "Again, I assure you: If two of you on earth agree about any matter that you pray for, it will be done for you by My Father in heaven. For where two or three are gathered together in My name, I am there among them."

"The church is one body," Ridnour says. "The church isn't made up of one person. It's a body of people that goes out into the world. Two or three are so much stronger than one, even in prayer. When you have more people on the same page together, it's much more powerful than when there's just one." This realization has pushed Ridnour and his wife, Kate, to get more involved in their local church and to find time for Christian fellowship. When the couple makes decisions, they ask others to help them pray beforehand. It's been an incredibly enlightening experience and has opened their eyes to the mighty force that is unleashed when biblical teamwork is engaged.

"The church is the place where everyone *should* pull together," Ridnour expounds. "Everyone has the same common goal. Everyone has the same prize in sight. When everyone is on the same page and everyone has the same vision and can see the same things, it makes it easier to guard against all of the attacks that the devil throws at you. Working as a team, the church can be a bigger force. It's like we're on a big battlefield and when we're all together, we're much stronger."

The Old Testament gives us many examples of people working toward a common goal. In one such story told in 2 Chronicles 28–31, God's people suffered through the ungodly rule of King Ahaz before his death opened the door for King Hezekiah. In order to bring the nation back to the Lord, Hezekiah began a long, arduous process that included cleansing the temple, renewing temple worship, celebrating Passover, and removing all of the idols brought in under Ahaz's rule.

The key to Hezekiah's success in restoring the people to God is found in 2 Chronicles 30:12: "The power of God was at work in Judah to unite them to carry out the command of the king and his officials by the word of the LORD." In other words, the nation had to come together and work as a team with one purpose in mind.

As a lifelong athlete, Ridnour has seen what happens when that singular vision isn't in place. "The worst that can happen in a locker room is when you have fighting going on," he says. "It makes it real tough. When there's no team unity, there's a lot of bickering and people talking behind each other's backs. That's not fun to be around. It's tough to win that way."

Ridnour's assessment lines up perfectly with Proverbs 29:18, where Solomon warns, "Where there is no vision, the people perish: but he that keepeth the law, happy is he" (KJV).

"When we're not together, it allows Satan to pick his way in," he adds. "If he can get one person going the wrong way, it just breaks everyone up. That's something we have to be careful about."

In that sense, Ridnour agrees that all believers at some level need to become spiritual point guards. We must all have a sense of our surroundings but never lose sight of the big picture. And that means building and nurturing friendships with the people who are pressing toward the ultimate prize—a relationship with Jesus both here on earth and forever in heaven.

"When you have people around you who are on the same page, you have that accountability that you need," Ridnour concludes. "You've got someone watching your back. It's easy to get sidetracked, and when you try to go solo, you might start doing things you shouldn't be doing. But when you have that fellowship of people and close friends who have the same vision with you, it makes it a lot easier. You know those people are there with you in the battle, and they're with you for the long run."

Training Time

1. Can you remember the very first team you were a part of? What was your role, and how did you contribute? What lessons did you learn in

your earliest experience with team-work?

2. Read Philippians 3:12–14. According to this passage, what are some qualities associated with good vision? How does knowing that you "have been taken hold of by Christ Jesus." make you feel? How does that promise impact your ability to focus on the prize?

3. How would you describe the perfect teammate, co-worker, or friend? What challenges have distracted you from fulfilling that role in the lives of others?

4. Read Proverbs 29:18. In what ways can you apply this verse to the team dynamic? What are some of the ways that you could promote a like-minded vision within your team?

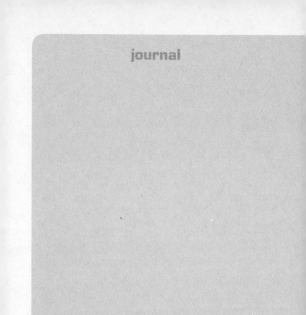

journal

6

All for One

TAMIKA CATCHINGS
WNBA Forward and Three-Time Olympic Gold Medalist

The body is not one part but many.

> 1 Corinthians 12:14

They said you have to use your first best player, but I found out you win with the five that fit together best.

> Red Auerbach

When Tamika Catchings was in the third grade, she played on her first basketball team alongside sister Tauja. Her father, Harvey Catchings—an eleven-year NBA player—was the coach of the squad that, other than his daughters, consisted only of boys. The fact that Catchings and her sister were the only girls on the team is interesting, but it's not nearly as telling as the principles they learned from their dad's coaching style. "We had to learn how to play as a group," Catchings recalls. "My dad always preached about how it was a team effort. We got that drilled in our head."

Maybe that's why Catchings, the All-Star forward for the WNBA's Indiana Fever, has never really struggled with the concept of teamwork. No matter how much individual success she has accrued on the basketball court, her number one goal has always been winning and doing it as a team.

Catchings was born in Stratford, New Jersey, in 1979 while her father was playing for the New Jersey Nets. He had previously played in Philadelphia. When he was traded to the Bucks, the family followed him to Milwaukee, where he played five seasons. When he played one final NBA season with the Los Angeles Clippers, the rest of the family remained in Milwaukee before moving to Italy, where he continued his career.

Tamika Catchings attended first grade at an overseas international school but moved back to Abilene, Texas, a year later, where she attended second grade. She then moved to Chicago, where she lived through her sophomore year in high school. During that time, her parents divorced, and she and her siblings stayed with their mother.

In Chicago, her athletic career started to blossom. As a sophomore in 1995, she was on Stevenson High School's Division AA State Championship team and was named Illinois Ms. Basketball. The following year, her mother moved the kids to Duncanville, Texas, where, as a senior, Catchings led Duncanville High School to a state title.

By then, the recruitment letters were steadily streaming into her mailbox. But as early as the eighth grade, Catchings had developed a strong desire to play for the University of Tennessee, after happening to notice Lady Volunteers' head coach Pat Summitt on a nationally televised game.

That's when everything changed.

In Knoxville, Catchings was an instant star. As a freshman, she played a key role on the team that went 39–0 en route to the 1997–98 NCAA national championship. By the time her college career was over in 2001, she had become just the fourth woman to be named First Team All-American in four consecutive seasons.

But her newfound national fame within the world of women's basketball wasn't the only major change in Catchings's life. She also found herself straying from some of the good habits she had learned as a child and teenager. "We grew up in the church," Catchings says. "Everything the church offered, we did. Our parents just made sure that we were always involved in some positive activity. Even though we got older and may have fallen off as far as going to church and doing the things we had grown up doing, we always ended up going back to it."

Admittedly, though, Catchings mostly neglected her spiritual needs during her first three years in college—that is, until she tore the anterior cruciate ligament in her right knee against Mississippi State on January 15, 2001.

"After I got hurt my senior year in college, it seemed like my need for a relationship with God became that much more obvious to me," Catchings says. "There was a huge chunk that was missing in my life that I was filling with basketball. Basketball was my god. Before the injury, I couldn't go to church because I had practice, or I had something else going on. I started to lose that balance that I grew up with. So after my injury, I got back to going to church; and then one thing after another, my faith continued to grow. It is who I am, and that's how I've come through adversity, knowing that I have Him to count on. It makes things that much easier."

Her renewed commitment to Christ also helped her solidify the true meaning of teamwork, which she had been taught at a very young age. "Teamwork is a group of people who come together to work for a common goal," Catchings says. "Whether it's winning a championship or whether it's getting a project done, they have a common goal, and everybody's on the same page."

As part of Tennessee's national championship team, Catchings caught her first glimpse of selfless team play. She shared the court with future WNBA stars Chamique Holdsclaw and Semeka Randall (now the head women's basketball coach at Alabama A&M), yet each of those top-tier athletes put aside their personal goals and worked to fulfill one singular vision. "All of us came together," Catchings says. "Some people had to sacrifice more than others, but we did it together as a team. It's not like one individual did it for the whole team."

Catchings says that the same was especially true of the amazing collection of athletes who made up the gold medal-winning women's basketball teams at the 2004 Olympics in Athens, the 2008 Olympics in Beijing, and the 2012 Olympics in London. All three squads went undefeated thanks to some of the greatest female hoops stars to ever grace the basketball court, including Lisa Leslie, Diana Taurasi, Tina Thompson, Sue Bird, and Kara Lawson.

"You get the best players in the USA," Catchings says. "All of us on our respective teams are the best players. You go from our teams in the WNBA to practicing for a few days and then winning a gold medal. People had to put aside their differences and understand that it's not about them. It's not about the Indiana Fever or whatever team they play for. This is about us getting together to win the gold medal, and that's what we did."

Sadly, those displays of true teamwork are not always prevalent, and many times individualism rises up and destroys chemistry between teammates. Catchings lists pride, ego, and a general inability to accept one's role as some of the primary enemies of teamwork. Ultimately, however, she believes that modern society's love affair with pop culture and fame may just be the biggest culprit.

"In this world, people put superstars on a pedestal—the rich, the famous, the sports stars," Catchings says. "So we're taught from a young age, 'That's who I need to be.' There are players who accept their roles, but there are a lot of players who want to be 'the woman' or they want to be 'the man.' That's where you struggle with teamwork, because you have players on the team who don't grasp the fact that they could win more games if everyone would just do what they're good at instead of trying to do everything."

Found on the reverse side of that coin is the dynamic created by athletes who covet more playing time, more recognition, or more respect. The desire is usually internalized at first, but if it is left unchecked, resentment will eventually bubble over into the locker room and have a potentially devastating impact on the rest of the team. For those struggling with the temptation to give in to that negative dynamic, Catchings has a simple solution.

"Work harder," she suggests. "Don't sit there and blame somebody else for what they're doing. You always hear the story about people who say, 'I'm waiting for God to do something in my life' while they're sitting on the couch at home. It's hard for God to make a move if you're not putting out the effort."

Another enemy of teamwork—which often accompanies individualism and is the root cause of covetousness—is jealousy. As Catchings has witnessed firsthand at various levels of competition, the words written in James 3:16 are all too true: "For where envy and selfish ambition exist, there is disorder and every kind of evil."

"Jealousy can destroy a team," Catchings says. "A lot of it comes from outside people saying, 'You can do this and you can do that' or 'The only reason you can't do it is because that other player is getting two more shots than you are.' It's funny when you think about it, but that happens, and then you start buying into it; and you start saying, 'Yeah, I should be playing more.' But whatever God has for you, you will have. Nobody can take that away."

It is Catchings's confidence in who she is and, more importantly, in who she is in Christ, that allows her to stay shielded from the jealousy, self-serving individualism, and prideful behavior that so predictably ravage the team concept. Her assurance can be traced back to the powerful passage found in Jeremiah 29:11: "'For I know the plans I have for you'—this is the LORD's declaration—'plans for your welfare, not for disaster, to give you a future and a hope.'"

Even with that understanding, Catchings admits to struggling with one of the more seemingly innocuous—though nonetheless deceptive—enemies of teamwork. Because of the high expectations that are placed on her as one of the WNBA's elite players, she must always stay alert to the danger of trying to do too much to help make up for what others aren't getting done.

"Sometimes when you try to cover up for other people's weaknesses, you end up doing more and more and more," Catchings says. "You look at Michael Jordan. When he started playing, he was doing everything. But once he figured out how to let his teammates help him, he won six championships. There's a fine line between trying too hard and not trying hard enough."

Like Jordan, Catchings has experienced a great deal of individual success in the professional ranks. After sitting out the Indiana Fever's 2001 season due to an injury, she returned in 2002 and won WNBA Rookie of the Year honors. In 2005, she scored her two thousandth point in the WNBA, reaching that mark faster than any other player had ever done in the league's history. Catchings also reached 1,000 rebounds, 400 assists, and 300 steals faster than any other WNBA athlete. Catchings has won a pair of Defensive Player of the Year awards (2005 and 2006) and was the leading vote getter for the 2006 WNBA All-Star Game.

Still, with all of those personal accolades and individual achievements, Catchings is most interested in team success and WNBA Championships, a goal that the Fever finally achieved in 2012. In order for those team goals to happen, she understands how important it is for all players to recognize the truth found in 1 Corinthians 12:12–14, where the apostle Paul compares a physical body to the body of Christ. In verse 12 of that passage, he explains that "as the body is one and has many parts, and all the parts of that body, though many, are one body—so also is Christ." He continues in verse 14 with this nugget of divine wisdom: "So the body is not one part but many."

"I can't win every game by myself," Catchings says. "The more that my teammates can do, the better off this team will be. When I can help somebody else and they can get a little bit of love, I don't care who scores the most points per game. At the end of the game, if we won and you scored more points than me, that's great."

Catchings has also learned that there is a rewarding aspect of teamwork that many people tend to overlook. Romans 12:10 says, "Be kindly affectionate to one another with brotherly love, in honor giving preference to one another" (NKJV). It's that last phrase, "giving preference to one another," that really stands out to Catchings, who—despite her knack for scoring lots of points—truly enjoys seeing her teammates shine.

"It's all about spending that extra time after practice with players who need to work on certain things," Catchings says. "I haven't always been a great communicator, but in becoming a leader for my team, it's like, *What can I do to help people?* The biggest thing for me is just constantly being in my teammates' ears—telling them what we expect from them and telling them what we need from them. Knowing that, I think any player will play better."

One of Catchings's favorite examples of teamwork in the Bible can be found in the lives of the twelve men that were called to be Jesus's disciples. This diverse group quickly learned that they were no longer looking out for their own self-interests but, as it says in Philippians 2:4, "for the interests of others."

"That's a huge step," Catchings says. "They were so close to God, and as disciples they had power to do so many different things. But at the end of the day, to be able to carry out His will and to be able to work together as a team, that's kind of awesome to think about."

When Catchings talks about the importance of serving within the confines of the team, she isn't just giving lip service or saying what people expect her to say. She has backed up her desire to lift others up to a higher understanding of teamwork through her Catch the Stars Foundation. The organization was birthed on the heels of a series of successful "Catch the Fever Camps" and "Catch On to Fitness Clinics."

"Our mission is to help kids catch their dreams one star at a time," Catchings says. "We have a mentoring program. We have a fitness program. But one of the things we always come back to is being able to work with other people. We put kids together who have never been together in their life. While they're at the camp, they're going to learn to work with that team and that person.

"You have to teach these things to kids at an early age," Catchings adds. "You look at these role models these days, and a lot of the athletes are not doing the positive things they should be doing. Even if you don't think people are watching, they're always watching."

Catchings believes that teamwork must eventually go well beyond the sports realm and carry over into every aspect of life—especially for those who have made the decision to accept Christ as Savior and Lord.

"There are so many people out there who challenge the Word," Catchings says. "They challenge Christianity. They challenge whether there's a God or not. That's why there are so many other religions, because people are looking for something else. That's why it's important for us to come together and unite. We need to gather as Christians. Our main goal is to praise God and to live our lives for Him and to please Him. It's not to please man, because like it says in the Bible, if you try to please man, you're always going to be disappointed."

Training Time

1. Have you ever been part of a team on which everyone was relatively equal in their level of talent? If so, what challenges did that present to the concept of teamwork?

2. What are some messages in our society that promote selfish ambition? Read James 3:16. What are some ways jealousy and selfishness can cause disorder and evil within a team's ranks? Have you ever dealt with a similar situation? If so, what

did you do to overcome the strife caused by these negative attitudes?

3. Catchings says that she enjoys watching her teammates excel. Read Romans 12:10. How does this attitude contrast with what you usually see exhibited by today's superstar athletes?

4. Read Philippians 2:1–4. What does the apostle Paul say are some key values necessary to keep a team focused on one goal? How should the admonition of verses 3 and 4 play out on the field or at work? How does the concept of putting others first translate to your role as a member of God's team?

5. Read John 13:35. According to Jesus, what is the significance of godly teamwork as it relates to reaching your world? In striving to live this teaching out in your life, what characteristics of Christ will you begin to pray for?

journal

Thanks

Fellowship of Christian Athletes would like to give honor and glory to our Lord and Savior Jesus Christ for the opportunities we have been given to impact so many lives and for everyone who has come alongside us in this ministry.

The Four Core values are at the heart of what we do and teach. Many people have helped make this series of books on these values a reality. We extend a huge thanks to Chad Bonham for his many hours of hard work in interviewing, writing, compiling, and editing. These books would not have been possible without him. Thanks also to Chad's wife, Amy, and his three sons, Lance, Cole, and Quinn.

We also want to thank the following people and groups for their vital contributions: Cat Whitehill, US Soccer Federation, Andy Pettitte, Randy Hendricks, Luke Ridnour, Tamika Catchings, Tauja Catchings, Kevin Messenger, and the Indiana Fever.

Thanks to the entire FCA staff, who faithfully serve coaches and athletes every day. Thanks to our CEO and president, Les Steckel, for believing in this project. Thanks to Jeff Martin, Shea Vailes, Julie Martin, and the entire National Support Center staff. Thanks also to everyone at Revell.

Impacting the World for Christ through Sports

Since 1954, the Fellowship of Christian Athletes has challenged athletes and coaches to impact the world for Jesus Christ. FCA is cultivating Christian principles in local communities nationwide by encouraging, equipping, and empowering others to serve as examples and make a difference. FCA reaches more than two million people annually on the professional, college, high school, junior high, and youth levels. Through FCA's Four Cs of Ministry—Coaches, Campus, Camp, and Community—and the shared passion for athletics and faith, lives are changed for current and future generations.

Fellowship of Christian Athletes
8701 Leeds Road
Kansas City, MO 64129
    www. fca.org
    fca@fca.org
    1-800-289-0909

Fellowship
of Christian Athletes
Competitor's Creed

I am a Christian first and last.

I am created in the likeness of God Almighty to bring Him glory.

I am a member of Team Jesus Christ.

I wear the colors of the cross.

I am a Competitor now and forever.

I am made to strive, to strain, to stretch and to succeed in the arena of competition.

I am a Christian Competitor and as such, I face my challenger with the face of Christ.

I do not trust in myself.

I do not boast in my abilities or believe in my own strength.

I rely solely on the power of God.

I compete for the pleasure of my Heavenly Father, the honor of Christ and the reputation of the Holy Spirit.

My attitude on and off the field is above reproach—my conduct beyond criticism.

Whether I am preparing, practicing, or playing, I submit to God's authority and those He has put over me.

I respect my coaches, officials, team-mates, and competitors out of respect for the Lord.

My body is the temple of Jesus Christ.

I protect it from within and without.

Nothing enters my body that does not honor the Living God.

My sweat is an offering to my Master. My soreness is a sacrifice to my Savior.

I give my all—all the time.

I do not give up. I do not give in. I do not give out.

I am the Lord's warrior—a competitor by conviction and a disciple of determination.

I am confident beyond reason because my confidence lies in Christ.

The results of my effort must result in His glory.

Let the competition begin.

Let the glory be God's.

© Fellowship of Christian
Athletes, 2016

Sign the Creed • Go to www.fca.org

Fellowship of Christian Athletes
Coach's Mandate

Pray as though nothing of eternal value is going to happen in my athletes' lives unless God does it.

Prepare each practice and game as giving "my utmost for His highest."

Seek not to be served by my athletes for personal gain, but seek to serve them as Christ served the church.

Be satisfied not with producing a good record, but with producing good athletes.

Attend carefully to my private and public walk with God, knowing that the athlete will never rise to a standard higher than that being lived by the coach.

Exalt Christ in my coaching, trusting the Lord will then draw athletes to Himself.

Desire to have a growing hunger for God's Word, for personal obedience, for fruit of the spirit and for saltiness in competition.

Depend solely upon God for transformation—one athlete at a time.

Preach Christ's word in a Christ-like demeanor, on and off the field of competition.

Recognize that it is impossible to bring glory to both myself and Christ at the same time.

Allow my coaching to exude the fruit of the Spirit, thus producing Christ-like athletes.

Trust God to produce in my athletes His chosen purposes, regardless of whether the wins are readily visible.

Coach with humble gratitude, as one privileged to be God's coach.

© Fellowship of Christian Athletes, 2016. Revised from "The Preacher's Mandate."

Impacting The World
For Christ Through Sports

Since 1954, the Fellowship of Christian Athletes has challenged athletes and coaches to impact the world for Jesus Christ. FCA is cultivating Christian principles in local communities nationwide by encouraging, equipping, and empowering others to serve as examples and make a difference. FCA reaches more than 2 million people annually on the professional, college, high school, junior high, and youth levels. Through FCA's Four Cs of Ministry—coaches, campus, camps, and community—and the shared passion for athletics and faith, lives are changed for current and future generations.

Fellowship of Christian Athletes
8701 Leeds Road • Kansas City, MO 64129
www.fca.org • fca@fca.org • 1-800-289-0909

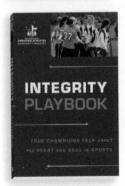